Contents

Aberdeen
A Celebration in Pictures

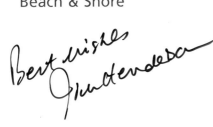

By Jim Henderson

Best wishes Jim Henderson

Preface & Acknowledgments

Approaching a book of this nature is a daunting task and it goes without saying that it is impossible to do justice to a city of Aberdeen's size and with its infinite variety of architectural styles in a book of 300 photographs. If the reader is unhappy with the selection then I accept all the blame but I hope that on balance I have pleased most of you. Pubs, hotels, shops and converted apartment blocks were too numerous to even be nibbled at; for another time perhaps.

Despite the great help and support at the final selection of the photographs by Susan and Jenny of Aberdeen Journals, the style and choice of the photography is very much down to myself as the photographer. A big thanks has to go to Bruce Irvine at the P&J for his Herculean task in changing my digital files into prints for making a much easier way of sorting through the photographs eventually used in the book.

Born in Torphins, my first association with the City was an unconscious one when I was taken from Banchory to Malaya at a few months old. One of my first and earliest conscious memories however was hitting the granite setts at the Railway Station when I fell out of a taxi at the tender age of 4! Later as a Banchory Academy pupil I travelled regularly on Saturday mornings for Art Classes at the Gray's School of Art on Schoolhill with journeys from Union Street by double-decker out to Banchory. A trip to the ARI accompanied by my uncle to have a finger X-rayed, and regular visits to Kepplestone Avenue on visits to his home are other childhood memories of Aberdeen. A deeply cherished event was as a junior golfer visiting Murcar for my first golf match outwith Banchory in a junior inter-club match in the 50's? I re-established my association with the City in the 1974 (W.J.Brown & Sons in Union Row; all changed now) and then working full-time in the oil industry until 1986, when I made a career change into professional photography.

My first link with Aberdeen Journals was their use of two of my photographs, in the 1988 P&J Colour Calendar; one was of Christmas decorations in Union Street. Since then I have regularly photographed the City, throughout its seasons, as the snow photographs in this book alone testify, and my photographs have been regularly used illustrating the City and Aberdeenshire?

What I think of the City will be said by my photographs. It will save you reading through many thousands of words!!

OK I know Aberdeen isn't like this all the time, blue skies and sunshine but do you really want to look at photographs of it in the rain, haar and on those wet, sleety grey miserable Christmas shopping days that we all know too well. Most of the photographs where taken in the space of five weeks this summer, so although it is a reflection perhaps of an unusually good summer, I can vouch that most years I have plenty of good photography opportunities in the city.

In the production of this book and the gathering of the photographs for it, there were many people involved in helping in all sorts of ways. I must thank them for their assistance and permission in granting access where applicable, as well as giving advice and putting up with the demands of a photographer often asking the unusual and inevitably changing his plans because of the weather.

Irene & Salvation Army for the Citadel views. Aberdeen City personnel, Derek and Jonathan at St Nicolas House, Martin at HM theatre, Deirdre at the Aberdeen Art Gallery and the staff at the Aberdeen Maritime Museum and Christine & staff at Provost Skene's House. Colin at Aberdeen Harbour Board and his Pilot Boat Staff for my fascinating trip to sea and around the Harbour and Tony for his 'seven trawler' incentive to make it a definite for the fish market at 5.00am in the morning. Neil, Curator at the Marischal College Museum for his advice on a difficult local choice to illustrate a small part of his wonderful, world-wide ethnic collection.

Les and Derek at Network Rail for their patience and stories of the Station and listening to mine of the days of the Banchory 'Sputnik' and The Aberdonian Kings Cross sleeper on which I travelled many times. Clare at Aberdeen Exhibition Centre and for what I have to admit was a rather 'space' age experience having photographed the site last in 1988!

Malcolm and Paul at Aberdeen Football Club and for letting me actually touch hallowed ground – first time I had ever been in the Pittrodrie Stadium, sacrilege to admit that I know.

Gerry, Kim, Hilary and Raymond at BAA and NATS for organising a plane spotters dream come true – shame it was cloudy but I must admit that the Aberdeen security checks have always outdone Heathrow, even for the Land Rover ride to the Control Tower? Shona for my tour to find the possible, non-building site photo of the new Sick Children's Hospital with the West Wing an Egyptian Temple as they might have been. Sarah at the Gordon Highlanders Museum and her 'hands on' exhibit?

Nick Saul and his staff at Northlink Ferries for their assistance in letting me use the upper deck of their ferry as a suitable way of capturing what I think, in a very gentle sense,

is the essential Aberdeen, still showing its solid character of decades gone past. I wonder what the City will be like in 100 years time – I suspect the granite will still be there?

The gardens included have many unsung heroes of course, especially those many staff who maintain the public parks which are featured in the book. These illustrate all the seasons of the year, as well as the fabulous displays of flowers gracing the City in the summer months, and which make it such a joy to photograph for my calendar stock every year. I might not so praise some of the various building changes, road signs, advertising and For Sale boards or awkwardly placed lamp posts and other normal city clutter but that is the challenge to any photographer.

The private gardens included were a mix of those I spotted on my travels and some were drawn from the Evening Express's garden competition. They were not chosen on any basis of merit, more for the desire to acknowledge some areas of the City that might otherwise have been neglected. I would like to thank all in this context for agreeing to let their gardens be used and especially I would like to thank Mary, John and Jack and the Rowett Institute for use of the garden that I experimented with to capture planes landing at the airport.

One timely surprise, received one week before Susan asked me to do the book, was the gift of some old photographs of Aberdeen and Royal Deeside from Lex and Dorothy de Booij in Holland. Dorothy is the daughter of the late Lionel Stuart, my golfing mentor at Banchory as a youngster, who was known to many North East Golfers for his immaculate attire as he officiated at many a Banchory golf match. The photographs were in a small album dated 1925, collected by a Jakul Ali, who served as a coachman at a Deeside house. I identified a small "JV" symbol and

thanks to Mrs Jackson at the James Valentine Archive at St Andrews University, I was able to confirm their origin. Their inclusion seemed very appropriate and gives an unusual glimpse of Aberdeen at around the turn of the last Century.

Mention should also be made of the books that I have had to hand to check some of my Aberdeen locations and descriptions. This is not a history book, and nor was it to be in the footsteps of another great book on Aberdeen, that of the late Alfred Eisenstaedt, which I won for an entry in the Aberdeen City Libraries' Focus on Aberdeen in 1989. His was essentially a 'people' book, mine isn't. I also recommend Aberdeen of Old by Edward Meldrum, The Granite City by Robert Smith, The Aberdeen Guide by Ranald MacInnes and Aberdeen, An Illustrated Guide by W.A.Brogden, the latter lent to me by Alison Ewan.

A huge thank you has to go to Susan McKay and Aberdeen Journals for offering me this chance of a lifetime and for trusting me with their important undertaking. Making proposals is all well and good but carrying them out is a different 'ball game'. This is especially so, when trying to capture the nature of any city, which is home to so many, and which will mean much in so many different ways to people all over the world who have a connection with this very special place, Aberdeen.

Jim Henderson
Kincardine O'Neil
26th September, 2003

City Centre from Citadel Tower

Aberdeen
City Centre

View down King Street
Castlegate from Citadel c1920's
Union Street from Citadel Tower
Citadel and Castlegate

Town House and Mannie Well
Queen Victoria's Statue in Townhouse
Mortification Boards in Townhouse

Pedestrian entrance to St Nicholas Centre
Sculpture detail by Gavin Scobie on Centre
St Nicholas Kirk from centre

Correction Wynd from Union Street
Kirkyard of St Nicholas Kirk
Oil Chapel in St Nicholas Kirk
Right Stained Glass window in St Nicholas Kirk

The Façade and Union Street c 1920's
Modern update of the photo above

Marischal College and Schoolhill
Little Belmont Street & Ma Cameron's
Trinity Centre Entrance off Schoolhill

Robert Gordon's from entrance archway
War Memorial at Cowdray Hall

Aberdeen Art Gallery Interiors of atrium of granite
columns with a glass doomed roof.

HM Theatre and view to Rosemount – a new addition in the pipeline
Springtime view over Union Terrace Gardens
Upper Union Terrace Gardens in winter light

Refurbished Statue of William Wallace
William Wallace Statue & HM Theatre c1920
Albert Statue in Upper Union Terrace Gardens

Union Terrace Gardens in rare snowy covering
Bon Accord Leopard for Christmas

Woolmanhill Hospital from Denburn Car Park
St Marks Church from Skene Terrace

Duke of Gordon Statue in Golden Square
Floral appreciation on Huntly Street Offices
Rubislaw Church and Queens' Cross Roundabout
Continental delights on Queen's Road

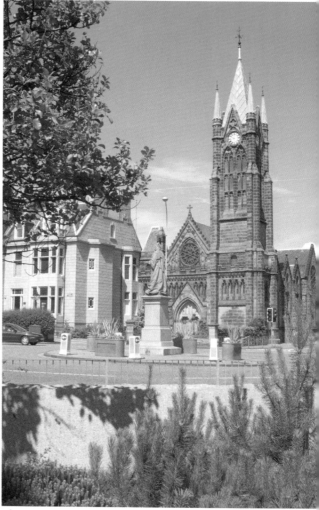

Albert Terrace from Carden Place
Rubislaw Quarry through hole in the fence

Viewfield Terrace roses display
The hidden charm of The Green below Union Street
Tree lined avenue opposite Gadie Crescent on Deveron Road near Springhill Park
Kaimhill and 'Deeside Way' from Auchinyell Rd

Graduation congratulations outside the Music Hall
Aberdeen Rowing Club prepare to launch on River Dee
Dreamy isolation

Union Bridge towards Union Terrace c 1920
Union Street looking West from Union Bridge

Aberdeen Maritime Museum from Shiprow
Museum interior of former Trinity Church looking over Harbour

Old trawlers medicine chest – a taste of the past
Drilling floor static display along with the other photos illustrate the industry that
now gives Aberdeen its ongoing prosperity, presented in the wide ranging
exhibits of this modern museum.

Robert Burns Statue in Union Terrace
Bryon's Statue at Grammar School
Nice for a hot day by Courts of Law
Edward V11 meeting spot on Union Street

Title "Duthie Park" Clydesdale Horses preparation and judging at Duthie Park, one of many activities that go on at this large park by the River Dee

Religious message through Pop at Mastrick Shopping Centre
Golfers enjoying sun baked grass and sea breezes at the Links Golf course, one
of many around the city.

Paul gets the Aberdeen Football Club Stadium at Pittodrie ready for the Rangers Match

Views around the City from The Citadel Tower
Union Street and West
View to Blaikies Quay and harbour entrance

View to Harbour Upper Dock and the South
View to Harbour entrance and River Dee Estuary

View past Virginia & Marischal Court to beach
View to Bridge of Don and the North

A few of Aberdeen's many churches: St Margaret's off Gallowgate, St Mary's RC Cathedral and a modern parish church at Summerhill.

City skyline from Greyhope Road thanks to modern zoom lens and great light
Time exposure looking down Union Street from Holburn Junction much to the
interest of several passing revellers.

Pilot Boat View Cruise Liner Leaving Berth

Aberdeen
Harbour

Activity near the RLNI Berth
Pilot Boat leaves Pocra Quay
Tradition passes the modern harbour lifeblood
The Islands' lifestock ferry frpm Pocra Quay

Pilot House from Silver Darling fish restaurant
A ferry approaches Pilot House in early morning sunlight

Ferry passenger view of Upper Quay fm MV Hrossey
Colourful telephoto view of city centre from Pocra Quay

Seafaring event of Tall Ships Race at Sunset
The Tall Ships Finale – the Fireworks Display

Strathelliot's crew offload latest catch before sun up
Fish Market in 'the good old days' c 1920's

Working routine from
inside the fishmarket

Colourful sunrise as backdrop to men at work
Winter evening departure for the fishing grounds

Pipehandler loading at ASCO Base fm Sinclair Rd
A Diving Support vessel like a sea-based 'Enterprise'

Soft summer sunset from Greyhope Road
Stormy sunset turns glorious as Rescue Boat comes home

Coast from Fittie play area

Aberdeen
Beach & Seashore

Continental style weather for a familiar beach cafe
Playing in the surf with haar at South Pier Light
Aberdeen Beach Promenade c1920's

Dawn peace on the winding road
Bright first light starts another day at the promenade
Flying on Cadona's Shockwave – a great way to mix the ice cream and hamburgers

Do I see a whale with Lourdes Cue's 'Windows to the Sea' situated near Donmouth?

Springtime by the Battery, looking to the harbour
Battery view up the coast to Seaton's highrises

Night-time UFO over the Battery and a fox for company
Dawn over the beach and a distant Girdleness Lighthouse

Girdleness Lighthouse and stormy seas c 1920's
South Pier in stormy sea action

Granite legacy sets off Girdleness Lighthouse
Some humourous graffiti and a foghorn

Dolphin action off the North Pier

MAX. SPEED LIMIT 5 KNOTS

Visitor watching for the dolphins by South Pier rocks
Dolphins seriously fishing at harbour mouth

Tide's out near Fittie's breakwater
Tide's out at Donmouth but are the fish running?

Fittie's Charm

Floral display in Union Terrace Gardens

Aberdeen
in Bloom

Upper Union Terrace Gardens in springtime
Union Terrace looking over the gardens
Aberdeen's Coat of Arms in the floral display
Rose Borders in Union Terrace Gardens with HM Theatre in the distance

Colourful respite from the shopping at St Nicholas Centre
Queens Terrace and Rubislaw Terrace offer a pleasant lunchtime break from nearby offices
Floral displays by the Kings Street Art Centre

At Riverside by the busy Bridge of Dee roundabout
City Centre from North Balnagask Road in Torry

One of the best years for the Rose Hill at Duthie Park

Peaceful Duthie Park and a perfect cuddle time
Duthie Park boating pond on a peaceful winter's evening
Colourful Duthie Park reminder that winter is over

Duthie Park bandstand against a winter sunset

May light and azaleas in Victoria Park
Victoria Park fountain with help from soft focus filter

Colourful welcome from Belvidere Street entrance
Victoria Park azaleas in full beauty
Victoria Park's famed Rhododendron Display

Busy part of Hazlehead Park with sad memories of an offshore tragedy at the Piper Alpha Memorial
A quiet thought or just watching the putting at Hazlehead

Fountain and many rose displays in Queen Mothers Rose Garden
Hazlehead Restaurant and children's payoff time
A riot of colour around the Hazlehead azalea borders

University Cruickshank Gardens
A hidden gem at Mugiemoss, the Persley Walled Garden

Seaton Park floral displays but also large playing areas on the banks of the River Don

Central floral display near St Machars Cathedral Kirk entrance

Autumnal colour by the Wallace Tower, part of Seaton Park at Tillydrone on the banks of River Don

Delightfully small Johnston Gardens off Viewfield Road with added vital attraction – accessible all year round public loo.

Johnston Gardens 1998 with good snow because of slightly higher location – a surprisingly rare sight like this in Aberdeen

Daffodil Time In Aberdeen
Bridge of Don
BP Offices at Dyce

Stronsay Drive
Riverside looking to Bridge of Dee
Union Terrace Gardens

Walks along the River Dee by Riverside Drive

Evening Roses on Great Southern Road

Aberdeen
Gardens in Bloom

Beechgrove Terrace near the famous TV gardens
Tough photography at this Ronaldsay Square garden

Interesting lines by this Auchinyell Road garden
Colourful front and back gardens with some thoughtful humour at Brimmond Place in Torry

English Cottage feel to this Balgownie Bridge Terrace garden
Mass of colour on Gordon Place in Bridge of Don

One of several of the Forrit Brae brigade – nothing like a bit of competition
Tradition kept up to scratch on Dalmaik Terrace in Peterculter

Marischal College from St Nicholas House

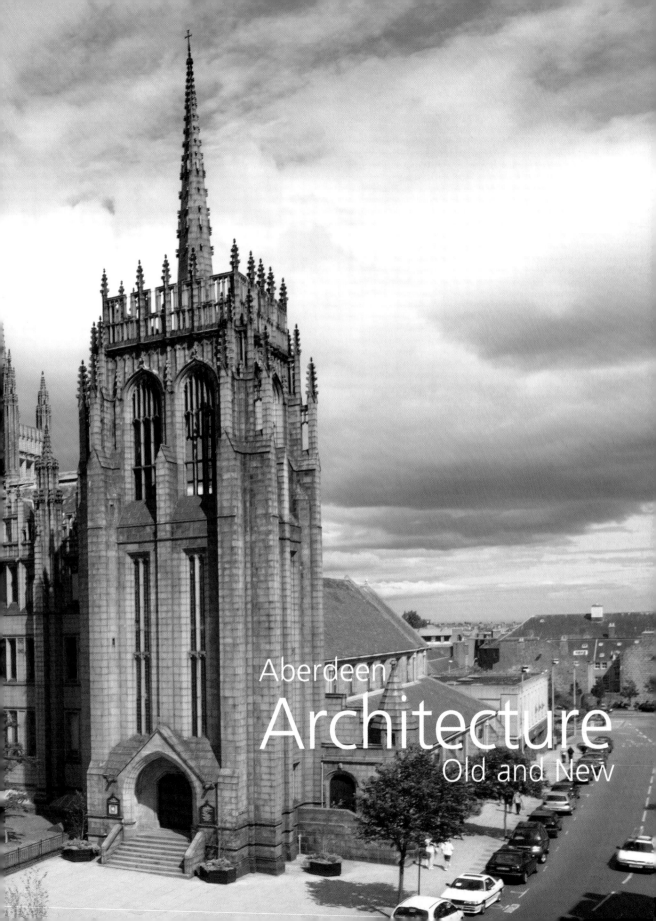

Aberdeen
Architecture
Old and New

Marischal College c1920's
Provost Skene's House

Marischal College Museum exhibit – James V Coat of Arms from old Aberdeen Mint but also a fascinating world wide ethnic collection
One of glories of Provost Skene's House is this well preserved and unique religious painted gallery
Water nymphs by Provost Skene's House
One of the painted panels in detail but no kilts!

Granite Style
Stirling Street & Carmelite Lane
Facing Trinity Street
Dee Street by the bakers shop
Rennies Wynd

Crown Street

Queens Road Casino at Dawn, an old style with modern exotic grace – would the architect have imagined it so? An old college probably green with envy, the ultra modern Talisman building on Holburn street

Classic Silver City Style at Bon Accord Crescent
The Tolbooth Spire, a 17Century legacy but still with a building elegance not matched much these days

West End Domestic Grandeur
Queens Cross Church & Roundabout
Gothic Impressions on Queens Road
Granite City Silver at Forest Road

Guild Street near the Harbour
A city by the sea – my favourite view from the Kings Gate
Railway Arches with tasteful upgrade
May clouds over George Street from Aberdeen College

Modern Industrial Styles of the Shell and Amerada Hess Buildings at Altens

An Evolution of Styles

Post War Modernism with Northern Hotel at Kittybrewster
Central Library & St Marks Church
Tasteful high rise Council flats at Seaton
By Abbotsford Lane, Ferryhill in evening light

Apartment blocks old & new at Bridge Street and Rennies Wynd
Sick Childrens' not yet completed but flying high

Gordon Highlanders Museum with exhibits the children can touch – try on a gas mask
Tree lined entrance to Woodend Hospital from Hazlehead

Classic Granite Style at Bon Accord Crescent
A set from a 'space city' at the Aberdeen Exhibition and Conference Centre at the Bridge of Don (opposite)

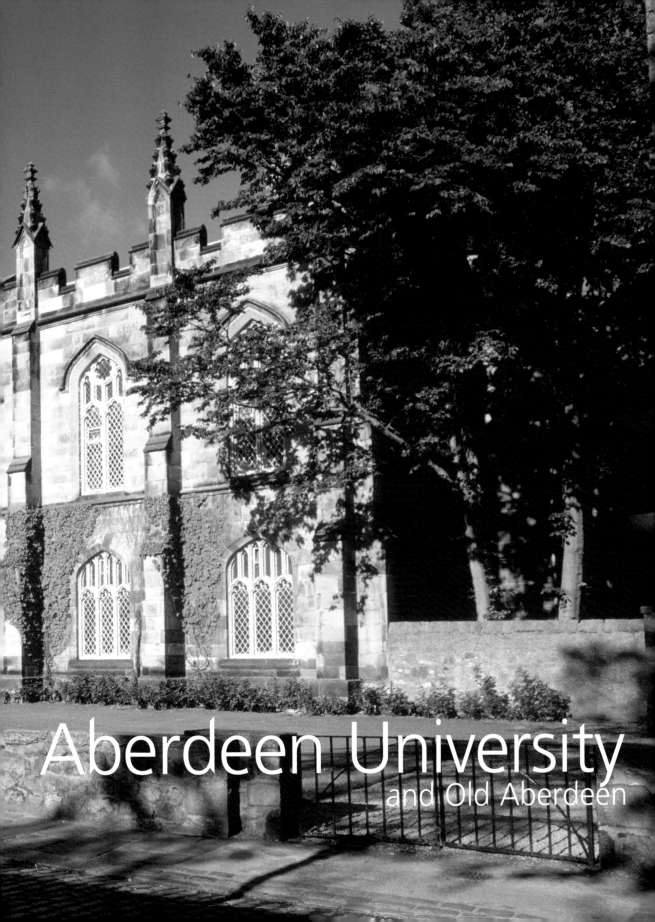

Aberdeen University

and Old Aberdeen

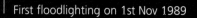
First floodlighting on 1st Nov 1989

Powis Gate Towers with an Arabian feel
Arched entrance into King's Quadrangle
The University for Harry Potter perhaps
New Kings

King's College c 1920's but dating from 1500
King's College Quadrangle

Kings Chapel and monument to the
University's founder, Bishop Elphinstone

Old domestic architecture of Old Aberdeen
Mitchell's Hospital dating from the early 1800's

The Town House and Market Cross of Old Aberdeen
Don Street

St Machar's Cathedral Kirk c 1920's
St Machar's Cathedral Kirk golden in evening light

An old but favourite view of the Cathedral and an early postcard of Aberdeen for J Arthur Dixon

The Fraser Noble building and The Queen Mother library

BA Heathrow flight on finals over Aberdeen with the River Dee below – lucky?

Aberdeen
Connections
& Curiosities

A pleasant surprise, the new and very spacious restaurant
Orderly departure for next offshore shift at Heliport
Busy time with fixed wing and helicopter traffic and the very day it had to be cloudy

Saturday morning 'Cyprus' landing over Greenburn Road at Bucksburn.
When I flew to Cyprus it was BEA to Heathrow but via Cromwell Road
and a change at Edinburgh

Aberdeen Station terminal through the wall of glass with its etchings of sailing ship and whale skeleton
City of Aberdeen – our own engine and a little artistic touch thanks to Photoshop

High Speed departure of the 14.55 nearing Ferryhill and some frantic camera work
1850 Railway Bridge & Craiginches Outline

Culter Burn & Rob Roy Statue

Aberdeen
Rural Links

Maryculter view to the east south of R.Dee adjacent to Peterculter and Milltimber
Looking over Milltimber and Peterculter from Contlaw, north of River Dee

Rural landscape at Milltimber with the distant spires of Blairs, former RC College south of the R. Dee
R Dee view to Milltimber from busy commuter road on South Deeside Road near Mill Inn
Very rural scene at Countesswells, on northern road into Cults

Shakkin Brig (Morison's Bridge) by Cults Burn and
the flood runoff with some naughty little footprints

Labour intensive land clearing scheme of mid-1800's called the Consumption Dyke at Kingswells
Forrit Brae, a quiet second or two on a very busy rural short cut to the airport
Spring view to City Skyline from Tyrebagger dual carriageway
Keith Rand's contribution is one of many hidden gems in Sculpture Walk in the Tyrebagger Woods

Springtime approach to the City from Westhill, just before the Aberdeen Crematorium
Autumn at Hazlehead through the beech avenue at Woodend Crescent

Lochnagar just visible over R Dee from Leggart Terrace near Bridge of Dee
Bridge of Dee at Leggart Terrace fm south bank

City skyline from West Tullos dual carriageway at Abbotswell Road
At the top of West Tullos Road is this southern view from Nigg and the
nearby Loirston Country Park has equally great views over Kincorth

R Dee and City from Banchory-Devenick at Tollohill on the old Causey Mounth

The City and Balnagask from May gorse on the Ness Heights
A colourful train heading south with Girdleness Lighthouse the last Aberdeen landmark

Donmouth c 1920's but a view now closed out by extensive mature tree cover
Brig of Balgownie c 1920's

Brig of Balgownie today from the footpath running to the Bridge of Don – about the only view due to increasing tree cover

The River Don at Dyce
Late afternoon over Seaton high-rises from Donmouth & spires of St Machars' visible at right
Winter sun over a peaceful empty Balmedie beach

A composite overlay of a Northern Lights display over Deeside on the 21st August 2003 and the harbour lights from Greyhope Rd on the 22nd – as near as I have got so far!